W9-CZN-750

Relationships

21st-Century Roles

A Young Woman's Guide to Contemporary Issues™

Relationships

21st-Century Roles

BETHANY BEZDECHECK

ROSEN
PUBLISHING®

New York

LONGWOOD PUBLIC LIBRARY

For my mother, Donna, who has graced our family with her kindness

Published in 2010 by The Rosen Publishing Group, Inc.
29 East 21st Street, New York, NY 10010

Copyright © 2010 by The Rosen Publishing Group, Inc.

First Edition

All rights reserved. No part of this book may be reproduced in any form without permission in writing from the publisher, except by a reviewer.

Library of Congress Cataloging-in-Publication Data

Bezdecheck, Bethany.
Relationships: 21st-century roles / Bethany Bezdecheck. — 1st ed.
    p. cm. (A young woman's guide to contemporary issues)
Includes bibliographical references and index.
ISBN 978-1-4358-3540-5 (library binding)
1. Interpersonal relations. 2. Family. 3. Friendship. 4. Man-woman relationships. I. Title.
HM1106.B49 2010
158.2—dc22

                                                             2009012065

Manufactured in Malaysia
CPSIA Compliance Information: Batch #TW10YA: For Further Information contact Rosen Publishing, New York, New York at 1-800-237-9932

Contents

COMMITMENT ROMANCE BOND FRIENDSHIP
FRIENDSHIP BREAK-UP COMMUNICATION
FAMILY GROWING DATING
LATIONSHIP

INTRODUCTION

Hollywood A-listers Ben Affleck and Matt Damon aren't just famous for being award-winning actors and screen-writers; they're also famous for being the best of friends.

Affleck and Damon grew up two blocks away from each other in Cambridge, Massachusetts. They met through their mothers, who both worked in early childhood education. The boys were inseparable from the time Damon was ten and Affleck was eight. Both dreamed of

BEN AFFLECK AND MATT DAMON OWE THEIR SUCCESS AS ACTORS IN PART TO THE STRENGTH OF THEIR RELATIONSHIP. THEIR FANS ADMIRE THEM NOT ONLY FOR THEIR TALENT, BUT FOR THEIR LOYALTY TO EACH OTHER AS WELL.

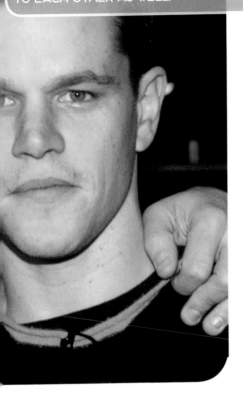

becoming actors and were active in high school theater together. At lunch, they would hold "business meetings" in the school cafeteria, during which they would discuss their plans of becoming real-live Hollywood movie stars.

At times, Affleck's and Damon's parents expressed concern over their desire to go into acting. They knew acting was a very competitive profession, and they didn't want to watch their sons endure too much rejection. Nevertheless, Affleck and Damon refused to give up their mutual dream. The encouragement and support with which they provided each other were stronger than any words of discouragement could ever be.

Although Affleck and Damon went to different colleges, they made a point to keep their friendship going strong. They visited each other whenever they could and spoke on the phone nearly every day. They continued to persuade each other that both had what it took to make it as professional actors, and they attended college theater courses in an effort to perfect their craft.

One day, Damon asked Affleck to give him some feedback on a scene he had written for a playwriting class. Always more than happy to help his best friend, Affleck eagerly reviewed the project. He was so impressed with the work Damon had done that he suggested they turn the scene into a full-fledged screenplay.

Some people would have laughed at the idea that their class project could become an actual feature film. Damon, on the other hand, didn't think twice about agreeing to his friend's proposal. He knew that when he paired up with Affleck, anything was possible.

The friends worked on their screenplay day and night. After college, they became roommates in New York and were able to complete their project side by side. They titled their screenplay *Good Will Hunting* and worked on selling it to a production company.

It wasn't long before Miramax Films bought the rights to *Good Will Hunting*. Affleck and Damon were thrilled by their success, but what was even more exciting was that they were going to star in the film. And just when they thought things couldn't possibly get better, famous director Gus Van Sant agreed to work on the movie, as did super-star actor Robin Williams.

Many people believed in the success of *Good Will Hunting*, but no one could have anticipated the magnitude of its eventual achievements. The movie opened to rave reviews and received two Academy Awards. Williams won the award for Best Supporting Actor, and Affleck and Damon accepted the award for Best Original Screenplay.

No one can deny that Affleck and Damon are talented actors and writers. However, it's the power of their relationship that has truly made them successful. It's doubtful that either of them would be where they are today if they hadn't continued to support and encourage each other. Their friendship is a perfect example of how working to maintain a strong, positive relationship can bring people happiness, success, and lifelong satisfaction.

You are not alone in your journey through life. No doubt you have friends and family members who believe in you as much as Ben Affleck and Matt Damon believed in each other. However, it takes a good deal of hard work and dedication to make the most out of any positive relationship.

ROMANCE FRIENDSHIP UNDERSTANDING COMMITMENT COMMUNICATION LIVING BOND FAMILY RELATIONSHIP

Relationships at a Glance

When most people hear the word "relationship," they think of a romantic couple. After all, everyday terms like "extramarital relationship," "relationship expert," and "long-distance relationship" have to do with this type of bond. However, there are many other types of relationships. A relationship is merely a connection between people, whether these people are boyfriend and girlfriend, father and daughter, or teacher and student. Therefore, since birth, you have been involved in a diverse collection of relationships.

Maintaining Relationships

We can all agree that relationships are extremely important aspects of our lives. Think about how much you depend on your friends and family, for instance. Without these relationships, you may not feel as loved or secure. Your happiness depends to a large degree on the well-being of your relationships, so you must never take them for granted. Every relationship, regardless of type, requires consistent communication, understanding, and consideration if it is to remain a part of your life.

To help you understand how to work on maintaining your relationships, here is a list of factors that can impact them:

1. Communication. In order for a relationship to survive, both parties must consider the other person's needs. Obviously, this requires a good deal of communication. To achieve an excellent level of communication, try to be open and honest with the people in your relationships. This way, they'll better understand your needs and how to support you. Meanwhile, when another person takes the time to be open and honest with you, be sure to really listen and to appreciate his or her effort to communicate.

2. Shared interests and activities. Many relationships exist because the people within them share a certain interest or activity. A shared activity can be anything from being on the same soccer team to simply living in the same household.

   Sometimes, relationships end because one person stops being engaged in the shared activity. If you've ever changed schools, you know what it's like to lose touch with people solely because you are no longer classmates. Still, some relationships can withstand changes in time, location, and interests. A friend who has moved away may still be someone with whom you speak on a regular basis.

3. Understanding. No two individuals are exactly alike. Therefore, people in a relationship must work hard to understand each other's point of view. Do you ever feel like your parents just don't understand where you are coming from? There's no doubt that if they made more of an effort to understand you, your relationship would most likely improve. Of course, relationships work

MOST RELATIONSHIPS ARE FORMED AS A RESULT OF SHARED INTERESTS AND ACTIVITIES. THE FRIENDS YOU MAKE WILL LIKELY BE THE PEOPLE YOU MEET WHILE IN CLASS OR TAKING PART IN ACTIVITIES LIKE SOCCER AND BAND.

both ways. You can't very well ask someone to be understanding toward you if you aren't being understanding toward him or her.

4. Caring and kindness. No one wants to have to put up with an unkind attitude. And if a person just doesn't seem to care about you, chances are, you'll stop caring for him or her. For these reasons, caring and kindness are beneficial

elements for the mere existence of any relationship. We would all like to be cared for and treated with kindness. If you ever find yourself in a relationship with someone who treats you poorly, sometimes you can work through the problem. Other times, particularly in an abusive relationship, the best course of action is to get out.

5. A common goal. Finally, in order for any relationship to survive, both parties may benefit from sharing a common goal. Some relationships between a boyfriend and girlfriend, for example, can exist only if both parties want to be exclusive and not date other people. A relationship between an employee and a manager may disintegrate if one person wants to see the company do well, while the other just wants to

WHEN YOU ARE FACED WITH A DIFFICULT SITUATION, IT HELPS TO HAVE SOMEONE CARING TO TURN TO FOR SYMPATHY AND ADVICE.

have fun. Understanding and communication will help you tell whether you and the people in your relationships want the same thing. If it turns out that you have different goals for your relationship, you'll need to work together to decide whether these goals can be modified. If not, the relationship may not last.

You may be thinking, "How can relationships be any fun at all if they require so much work and I have to be perfect?" Well, for one thing, you should only be required to do half the work it takes to maintain a good relationship. The second half should be provided by the other person involved. As your relationship grows and improves, doing your part will come more naturally to you. Also, keep in mind that part of a healthy relationship is being able to let go and have a little fun once in awhile. Taking everything too seriously will only cause stress for you and those around you.

DEALING WITH STRESSFUL RELATIONSHIPS

It is a sad fact that most people have issues that prevent them from having ideal relationships. That's why, for both teens and adults, learning how to maintain healthy relationships is a lifelong work in progress. There are parents, significant others, and even authority figures like bosses and principals who have

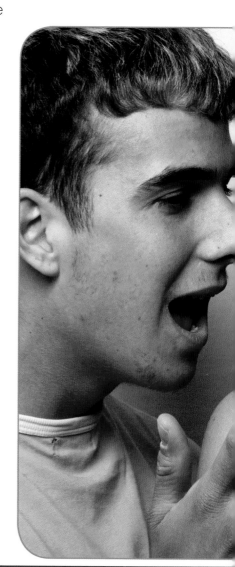

such a difficult time handling their own personal problems that they end up taking their frustration out on others. If you find yourself in a relationship where you are being physically or verbally abused, it's important to find a way out. This can be easier said than done, of course, especially if the person who is causing you grief is a member of your own family. However, escaping an abusive relationship is a must, for staying in one can only have disastrous effects. If

JUST BECAUSE YOU'RE NOT BEING HARMED PHYSICALLY DOESN'T MEAN YOU'RE NOT BEING ABUSED. IF SOMEONE IS CONSTANTLY PUTTING YOU DOWN IN A CONSCIOUS EFFORT TO MAKE YOU FEEL BAD, YOU'RE A VICTIM OF VERBAL ABUSE.

ROMANCE FRIENDSHIP UNDERSTANDING COMMITMENT COMMUNICATION WING BOND FAMILY RELATIONSHIP

you are having a trying time with any sort of relationship, don't be afraid to turn to one of the following people or organizations for help:

1. A school counselor. School counselors can help you achieve your best. Earning good grades and nurturing your academic interests can be very difficult if you don't have the support of your friends and family. School counselors are trained to help students who are dealing with troubled relationships. If you make an appointment to speak to one about the difficulties with which you are dealing, you can rest assured that the counselor won't share the information you tell him or her unless he or she feels your life or someone else's is in danger.

2. Crisis centers. A crisis center consists of a group of highly trained individuals who assist people in

DON'T BE AFRAID TO MAKE AN APPOINTMENT WITH A SCHOOL COUNSELOR. SCHOOL COUNSELORS HAVE CHOSEN THEIR PROFESSION BECAUSE THEY CARE STRONGLY ABOUT ASSISTING STUDENTS LIKE YOU.

coping with problems like physical abuse or drug and alcohol addiction. You can easily obtain a list of crisis centers in your area from the Internet, the library, or a school counselor. Phone calls made to crisis centers are kept private, so if you place a call to one, you need not worry about others finding out. A counselor may refer you to a crisis center if he or she feels your situation is an

emergency. If you have contemplated suicide or if you feel your life is in danger, it is best to call a crisis center, as the people working there can see to it that you receive the help you need right away.

3. Licensed psychotherapists. Licensed psychotherapists are clinically trained professionals who work with individuals looking to improve themselves and their relationships. Compared to

GROUP THERAPY SESSIONS OCCUR BETWEEN A LICENSED THERAPIST AND A GROUP OF PEOPLE COPING WITH SIMILAR PROBLEMS. ATTENDING GROUP THERAPY IS A GREAT WAY TO OBTAIN SUPPORT FROM PEOPLE WHO TRULY UNDERSTAND YOUR SPECIFIC SITUATION.

school counselors and crisis centers, therapists may be in a better position to give you their full attention for an extended period of time. Some therapists work in what is known as private practice, meaning they are not affiliated with a larger organization. These therapists usually charge money for their services, and you will likely need your parents' help to see one.

LONG-DISTANCE RELATIONSHIPS

A romantic relationship that takes place between two people who live a great distance apart is known as a long-distance relationship. It's normal for two people to lose touch when one of them moves away. Therefore, a common assumption about long-distance relationships is that they hardly ever work out. However, research shows that the breakup rate of couples in long-distance relationships is the same as that of couples who are geographically close. This is most likely because it takes a very committed, hard-working couple to endure a long-distance romance.

However, other therapists work out of hospitals and clinics, and they may offer their assistance at a reduced cost, or, in some cases, for free.

Therapy sessions can occur between just you and the therapist, or they can occur in groups. A group therapy session is a meeting of people dealing with the same type of issue, such as coping with the loss of a loved one or escaping domestic violence. These sessions are usually led by a licensed therapist, and only those who want to share that day will be requested to do so. Participating in group therapy may sound awkward or embarrassing to you, but it can actually be very helpful. If you attend a group therapy session, you will likely be relieved to meet others in your situation, and you will have the opportunity to develop new, caring relationships with these people.

Some people decide they'd like to work on their relationships together. For these especially motivated parties, family and couples therapy is available. Sometimes, one person in a relationship has to work to convince the other person or people that going to therapy together is a good idea. This is because many people are initially reluctant to get into counseling for a number of reasons, including fear or denial. What these people don't realize is that it often takes an objective third party to help people see a relationship clearly, especially when strong personal feelings are at play.

Seeking outside help with your relationships is not something to be ashamed of. It takes a strong, motivated person to put forth this type of effort. If more people were brave enough to ask others for help, the world would likely be a much happier place.

You can never have too many positive relationships, as long as you make sure to have enough time for everyone. Every relationship deserves your full attention, whether it's with a classmate or a coach. No one likes to be ignored or taken for granted. Read on to learn how to best take care of the following types of relationships: family, friends, romantic relationships, and most important, your relationship with yourself.

ACTIVE LISTENING

Active listening is a technique people use to become better communicators. Communication is just as much about listening as it is about talking. Listening actively helps you understand exactly what it is the other person is trying to convey. Active listening involves:

■ Repeating what the other person has just said, but in your own words. In doing this, you are proving to the other person that you have been making a conscious effort to listen to him or her.

■ Making eye contact with the other person while he or she is speaking, rather than exhibiting disinterest by fidgeting or focusing on something else.

EYE CONTACT IS AN EASY WAY TO SHOW A PERSON WITH WHOM YOU ARE COMMUNICATING THAT YOU ARE SINCERELY INTERESTED IN WHAT THEY HAVE TO SAY. IT ENCOURAGES THAT PERSON TO OPEN UP TO YOU.

- Encouraging the other person to keep communicating with you by asking positive, nonthreatening questions.
- Waiting a few moments before speaking yourself, in order to be sure not to interrupt.

MYTHS and Facts

MYTH

A good relationship shouldn't require any work; getting along should come naturally to the people involved.

Fact

All relationships require work. It is impossible for any two people to see things in the exact same way. Therefore, it's important that both parties in a relationship work hard on communicating effectively.

MYTH

The actions of parents, teachers, and other authority figures must never be questioned.

Fact

No one, no matter what his or her age or stature, should have to put up with a hurtful relationship. If a parent, teacher, or other authority figure is showing you disrespect, don't let that person's behavior slide. Explain the situation to a trustworthy adult, and allow him or her to help you decide what is to be done.

Myth

If you love your boyfriend, you should be willing to take your relationship to a physical level.

Fact

Just because you care for someone doesn't mean you should be ready to engage with him in sexual activity. The decision to have sex involves more than just emotions, and it should never be taken lightly. If someone is pressuring you to have sex, know that in doing this, he is being anything but loving.

CHAPTER 2

RELATIVE RELATIONS

You've probably heard the saying, "You can choose your friends, but you can't choose your relatives." These words are a reminder that while we can happily handpick our friends based on their personalities, likes and dislikes, and sense of humor, no matter how little we feel we have in common with our family members, we're stuck with them.

This notion may seem gloomy at times, but being stuck with someone isn't all bad. Remember, while friends come and go, family is forever. No matter where you are or what life brings your way, your family members will be a part of your life.

From talking with your friends, you probably know it's not unusual for family to get on a teenager's nerves. Family members can be embarrassing, nagging, and annoying, and the worst part is, they're always around! But have you ever asked yourself how you might come across to your family? Are you kind and courteous, or do stress and

Family reunions and get-togethers often evoke an atmosphere of love and togetherness. Despite their many differences and occasional disagreements, family members can't help but share a special bond.

ROMANCE FRIENDSHIP UNDERSTANDING COMMITMENT
OVING BOND FAMILY RELATIONSHIP COMMUNICATION

irritability sometimes make you difficult to be around? Remember, relationships work both ways, and it's not fair to ask others to change their behavior toward you unless you're willing to do the same for them.

Another phrase you may have heard is, "Someone needs to be the bigger person." When people are at odds, someone may need to step up and make things right. Otherwise, the anger and hurt feelings may go on forever. If you can sometimes be that person for your family, your parents and siblings may be motivated to follow your good example. In addition, they may be impressed by your actions and may therefore pay you more respect. Earning respect from your family is very important. When people respect you, they are more likely to trust you to make your own decisions.

Many families make a point of having dinner together. Because family members often have busy, conflicting schedules, dinner can be the one time each day they have to connect.

FRIENDSHIP UNDERSTANDING COMMITMENT
ROMANCE BOND FAMILY RELATIONSHIP
COMMUNICATION

Maintaining a Peaceful Family Environment

Of course, being the first person to take a step toward household peace is easier said than done. When your parents are quizzing you about your grades and complaining that you rarely help out around the house, chances are you'll feel more like screaming than being the bigger person. Thankfully, there are some useful tips and tricks for getting through such initial frustration.

First, see it from their side. Different members of a family see things completely different ways. While this alone can cause disagreements, it's forgetting this simple fact itself that keeps people from making amends. In order to effectively communicate, families must first recognize that each member has a unique point of view.

Because your parents or guardians care so much about your well-being, they can seem preoccupied with things like your schoolwork and safety. To them, keeping a close eye on these matters means being a cautious and compassionate caregiver. However, you likely find your parents' prudent actions overbearing, obnoxious, and unnecessary. It may be that in your mind, you're too old to need someone watching over you constantly. You may also feel your parents are being unsympathetic by thinking only of your curfew and grades, while ignoring those things that make you truly happy, like your social life and extracurricular interests.

With such different viewpoints, you and your family members may never completely see eye-to-eye.

However, you can at least try to understand one another's perspectives. If your parents are able to see how you can be negatively affected by their actions, they may think twice before doing something that could upset you. Meanwhile, you'll be less likely to get so angry with them once you recognize that their nagging ways may only be motivated by compassion.

Second, resist anger. When family members cause you stress, your first reaction may be to fight back. Such a reaction is perfectly natural, as fighting makes people feel better by allowing them to release their negative emotions. In the long run, however, anger will only make a situation worse.

Most adults see an angry outburst as being a sign of immaturity. Therefore, if you react to what you feel is an unfair situation by yelling at your parents or giving them the silent treatment, the only thing you'll be proving to them is that you're too immature to be taken seriously. While everyone deserves to be listened to, your parents or guardians may only take in what you have to say if you present your thoughts in a calm, respectful manner.

And last, learn the art of compromise. No one person should be allowed to have his or her way all the time. Of course, most people prefer things to go their way, and some will start arguments in an effort to get what they want. To prevent such fights from impairing your relationships, it's important to learn the art of compromise.

Compromising means coming to an agreement through which both parties get their way in exchange for a small sacrifice. As an example, let's say you and your older sister both want to use the family car. Your sister wants to drive to the library to return some books, then go to the mall to pick up a pair of boots she's had her eye on. You, on the other hand, have a friend coming over and would like the car so you can rent a movie for the two of you to watch. You'd also like to drive by the drugstore to buy some cosmetics. Neither of your schedules permits you to use the car at a later time.

Instead of causing hurt feelings by fighting over the car, you and your sister can compromise by riding together. If the two of you don't have time to complete all four tasks, you can each select the one that is most important to you and save the other for a later date. Doing this means neither of you will completely get your way, but you can both agree that it's better than one of you not being able to use the car at all.

COMPROMISE CAN BRING PEOPLE CLOSER TOGETHER BY GIVING THEM REASONS TO COMMUNICATE, SHARE, AND RESPECT EACH OTHER'S NEEDS, EVEN WHEN THE MOST CHALLENGING PROBLEMS ARISE.

AGE DIFFERENCE

Disagreements between family members are at times the result of age differences. This can be especially obvious when dealing with your parents. As a teenager, you're at a time in your life when it is important to you to be independent. Meanwhile, your parents are at an age

FORGETTING OR REFUSING TO TAKE A FAMILY MEMBER'S POINT OF VIEW INTO ACCOUNT WILL DRIVE A WEDGE BETWEEN YOU. MAKE A CONSCIOUS EFFORT TO COMMUNICATE WHENEVER POSSIBLE.

when their biggest concern is your safety. The result is that while you want to make decisions on your own, your parents want to know exactly what you're doing at all times. Needless to say, these different desires don't mix.

Age differences between siblings can also be a cause of family arguments. Younger siblings might admire their older siblings and look for reasons to be around them, while older siblings might want their space.

People of very different ages don't always see situations the same way. Therefore, everyone in your family needs to take extra steps to understand one another's point of view. Be the bigger person and remind your family members that it's natural for you to have your differences, and encourage them to allow everyone the opportunity to express their opinions.

As you grow older, you may find that your family relationships improve. An older brother who once found you a nuisance may discover that now you've matured, he has more in common with you and wouldn't mind hanging out with you once in awhile. One day when you move out on your own and no longer have to answer to your parents or guardians, you may find you are less annoyed by them. Until these changes occur, however, maintaining good family relationships will require working to see things from other family members' perspectives, trying to manage your anger, and learning to compromise.

⚥ GENERATION GAP

You, your parents, and your grandparents are all from different generations. A generation is a group of individuals born around the same period of time. Different generations have grown up in very different ways. If your grandparents are between the ages of sixty and eighty, they were your age during a time when people of different races were not considered equal in the United States. They also endured the Cold War, a period of tension between the United States and the Soviet Union that caused great levels of suspicion and anxiety. If your parents were born in the 1960s or 1970s, they're known as members of Generation X. This generation grew up in very stable times compared to those of their parents. As teenagers, members of Generation X rebelled against the more conservative ideologies of the past. Did you know your generation is referred to as Generation Y? What do you think it will be remembered for? It's up to you and your peers to make sure your generation is looked upon positively.

Differences in generations naturally cause differences in personalities and outlooks on life. They are therefore another source of tension within families. However, these differences don't have to cause conflict, as long as families remember to keep them in mind when communicating.

YOUR EXTENDED FAMILY

Family relationships can be more difficult to manage when it comes to your immediate family—your parents and siblings. Getting along with extended family—aunts, uncles, cousins, and grandparents—is usually easier. This is because these family members aren't around you as much

Writing a letter to a faraway relative is an excellent way to bring the two of you closer. The relative will likely appreciate your effort.

FRIENDSHIP UNDERSTANDING COMMITMENT
ROMANCE COMMUNICATION
WING BOND FAMILY RELATIONSHIP

and are therefore less likely to get on your nerves. Plus, you don't need to worry about seeking their approval. They don't have control over your actions the way your parents do. At the same time, if you're like most people, you're actually closer to your immediate family than you are to your extended family. The reason for this is, because you don't see your extended family as often, you probably know less about them.

Even though you may not see your extended family members every day, it's a good idea to work on building these relationships. Solid relationships with extended family members can be very rewarding. They will help you better enjoy large family get-togethers, and if you ever find yourself in a situation in which you need to depend on an aunt, uncle, or grandparent, you will feel more comfortable doing so if you are close to that person.

It's easy to improve relationships with extended family. Your extended family members have watched you grow up, and for this reason alone, they are invested in your well-being. They may appreciate you making an effort to get to know them better. Here are some ways in which you can become closer to your extended family:

1. A couple times a year, send a handwritten note to extended family members who do not live nearby. Older relatives especially enjoy handwritten cards, which they probably rarely receive since the invention of e-mail. Thank-you notes for birthday or holiday gifts are the perfect opportunity for showing your extended family you care.

FAMILY AROUND THE WORLD

In some cultures, it's common for immediate and extended family to live together. For example, in China and Korea, it's traditional for adult sons to bring their wives to live with them and their parents and grandparents. When daughters marry, they move in with the extended families of their husbands.

As more people from around the world are moving from rural areas to live in big cities, the number of extended families living together continues to decrease. At the same time, however, it is consistently common for the elderly to move in with their sons and daughters once they can no longer care for themselves. This is becoming increasingly common in the United States.

2. Learn about your genealogy, or family tree. Discovering where you came from and who your ancestors were is always interesting. Ask your extended family members for help. They will be able to tell you about relatives you are too young to have known.

3. Ask your grandparents what life was like when they were your age. It's fun to imagine your grandparents as teenagers, and older people enjoy reminiscing about their youth.

BLENDED FAMILIES

In addition to immediate and extended family, many people have stepfamilies. With the divorce rate on the rise, more than half of today's teenagers have stepparents. These relationships can be particularly stressful. If one of

ADOPTION, DIVORCE, AND THE RESTRUCTURING OF CIVIL RIGHTS LAWS HAVE RESULTED IN MORE DIVERSITY AMONG FAMILIES. AMERICANS ARE INCREASINGLY ADOPTING CHILDREN FROM OVERSEAS, MAKING FAMILIES OF DIFFERENT ETHNIC BACKGROUNDS FAR MORE COMMON.

your parents remarries, you may feel it's unfair to be expected to treat a strange, new adult like one of the family. However, no one is asking that you love your new stepparent more than you love your biological mother or father. The most that is expected from you in dealing with a stepparent is to try to understand that person's point of view.

Adjusting to stepfamilies is difficult for adults, too. Stepparents never intend for their current marriage to hurt anyone, especially their children. Their main objective is to simply enjoy time with their chosen life partner. However, they can't help but be concerned that their new stepsons or stepdaughters will resent them. If you have a stepmother or stepfather, it may help you to remember

FRIENDSHIP UNDERSTANDING COMMITMENT
ROMANCE BOND FAMILY RELATIONSHIP COMMUNICATION

that he or she is just as confused and concerned by the relationship as you are. So it is best to be patient with each other as everyone adapts to the changes in your family.

It's natural for teens to want to spend more time with friends than family. Your friends are closer in age to you, and you picked them because of how much you have in common. However, you may be surprised to find that you enjoy being at home if you have a comfortable family relationship. Family is forever, and strong family bonds are everlasting gifts.

Ten Great Questions
TO ASK A SCHOOL COUNSELOR

1.
What are some signs of being in an unhealthy relationship?

2.
How can I balance my relationships with my schoolwork?

3.
Can you recommend any resources on dealing with an unstable relationship?

4.
How can I manage the stress that comes with my relationships?

5.
Are there any after-school programs at which I can make new friends?

6.
Do you know of any teachers who might serve as a mentor to me?

7.
What are some things I can say to a friend who has fallen victim to peer pressure?

8.
How can I go about seeing a therapist?

9.
Do you have a list of local crisis centers?

10.
How can I talk to my parents about my relationships?

DATING UNDERSTANDING COMMUNICATIO
ROMANCE FAMILY COMMITMENT
BOND RELATIONSHIP
GROWING HONESTY
FRIENDSHIP BREAK-UI
SELF-ESTEEM

CHAPTER 3

WITH FRIENDS LIKE THESE

As a teenager, you rely on your friends a great deal. Usually, it's your friends who understand you best. Younger brothers and sisters aren't mature enough to relate to their teenage siblings, and adults have often forgotten what it was like to be a teenager. Therefore, it's important for you to have a great group of friends by your side.

Most people, regardless of age, look for the same qualities in a friend. These qualities include:

- **Loyalty** A loyal friend is someone who would try to avoid hurting you. A loyal friend values your friendship and understands that in order to maintain it, she should try to be honest and be more understanding.
- **Kindness** Of course, kindness is a necessary quality in a friend. Care and compassion are important qualities.

Having good friends means having fun, which reduces stress and improves your overall quality of life. Therefore, positive friendships actually play a big part in keeping you not just happy, but healthy, too!

- **Respect** Good friends deserve respect. No matter how close two people become, they should not take each other for granted. A long-lasting friendship means long-lasting respect.
- **Empathy** An empathetic friend is someone who tries to understand your emotions. When you're going through a tough time, she will sympathize with you and try to help you feel better. When you succeed, she will be happy for you and help you celebrate. A friend with whom you can share your ups and downs is a friend with empathy.
- **Common interests** It's fun to have friends who share your interests. You can talk to them about the things that excite you and take part in activities together.
- **Similar personality traits** People with similar personalities get along better because they find it easier to relate to each other. So it's typical for good friends to have similar personalities.

If you want your friends to possess the above qualities, you need to make sure you possess them as well. Of course, you can't be expected to have control over your interests or personality traits, but you need to be respectful and kind toward your friends if you want them to treat you the same.

MAKING FRIENDS

Moving to a new town, switching to a new school, or joining a new organization like a sports team or youth symphony means having to make new friends. If you find this concept stressful, you're not alone. Even adults experience anxiety over making new friends. When you're the "new person," you worry about not fitting in and figure that since everyone else already has a group of friends, they won't be interested in including one more person. Of course, such a defeatist attitude won't make you friends. It's better to recognize that in order to assist your social life, you may have to step outside of your comfort zone. In other words, you'll have to do a few things that may feel uncomfortable at first, like asking a group of girls if you can sit with them at lunch or striking up a conversation with someone whose company you think you'd enjoy. You may feel nervous and awkward doing these things in the beginning, but once you've successfully formed some new friendships, you'll wonder what you were once so scared about. The truth is, most people are interested in building new friendships, and most people will be able to sympathize with your situation. So don't be afraid of assertively seeking friends. You'll thank yourself later on.

THE RIGHT AND WRONG REASONS

It's not uncommon for teens to choose friends for the wrong reasons. More often than not, these reasons have to do with popularity. As a teenager, popularity can seem immensely important. You are working to create an identity for yourself through the clothes you wear, the music you listen to, and the people you hang out with, and you are relying on your peers to tell you whether this identity is acceptable. The more popular you are, the

more you can rest assured that others approve of your persona.

Because forging an identity can be frustrating, some teens choose to rely on others to create one for them. They seek out friends who are already popular because they know associating themselves with these people will make

JOINING A TEAM OR CLUB WON'T AUTOMATICALLY WIN YOU FRIENDS, ESPECIALLY IF YOU'RE NEW TO THE GROUP. PUT ON A FRIENDLY FACE AND SHOW INTEREST IN OTHERS, AND YOU MIGHT BE SURPRISED BY THE RESULTS.

them seem cooler. Of course, in doing this, they are denying themselves the opportunity to get to know their true selves. This isn't a good idea because while friends may come and go, you're with yourself for life.

If you choose your friends for popularity and not loyalty, kindness, and respect, you can't expect to have a very good support system. Someone who cares more about your social status than about your feelings isn't likely to help you up when you're down. At times, it may seem like popularity will make you happy, but if being popular means not having true friends, it's more likely to make you miserable.

DISAGREEMENTS AND GROWING APART

The friends you make for the right reasons have the potential to stay with you for a lifetime. However, it's important to understand that sometimes even the best of friends can grow apart. People change as they grow older. They develop different interests, move to different areas, and come to want different things from life. If you should find yourself

When involved in a disagreement between friends, it's important not to let anger get the best of you. This may mean walking away from a situation and giving each other some space for awhile.

FRIENDSHIP UNDERSTANDING COMMITMENT
ROMANCE COMMUNICATION
WING BOND FAMILY RELATIONSHIP

growing apart from a friend, recognize that no one is to blame. Such occurrences are perfectly natural, and there's no good reason to get upset over this type of situation. Also remember that nothing can take away the good memories you have from when you and your friend were closer, and just because a friendship changes, it doesn't mean it's over. Treasure your friendships, both for what they were and for what they are today.

Just as it's normal for friends to grow apart, it's normal for friends to have disagreements. Have you ever been upset with a friend for one of the following reasons?

1. You're crushing on the same guy. It's a given that friends with similar interests and personality traits will be attracted to the same type of people. Of course, this can lead to some unfriendly competition. What will happen if you and a friend of yours end up liking the

DATING ROMANCE FRIENDSHIP UNDERSTANDING COMMUNICAT GROWING BOND FAMILY RELATIONSHIP same boy? Many girls respond to this sort of predicament by trying to outdo each other and hurling accusations back and forth. In the end, it may not be that either of them has won the guy's approval, but one thing is for certain: their friendship has been destroyed.

What is the appropriate way, then, to deal with this type of situation? Should you simply

JEALOUSY IS A PERFECTLY NATURAL EMOTION. BUT DON'T ALLOW YOUR FEELINGS TO TURN INTO ANGER. IF YOUR FRIEND'S NOT OUT TO HURT YOU, SHE DOESN'T DESERVE LESS THAN KINDNESS AND SUPPORT.

ROMANCE FRIENDSHIP UNDERSTANDING COMMITMENT
WING BOND FAMILY RELATIONSHIP COMMUNICATION

swallow your true feelings and let your friend go after the boy you like? If doing so would cause you pain and resentment, then the answer is a definite no. You need to be fair to yourself, as well as fair to your friend. Since it's unlikely that your friend would stand by and just watch you pursue the boy either, there is but one solution to this common conundrum: you must remember to put your friendship first.

Undoubtedly, you and your friend will have a difficult time putting aside your love interest. However, it's important to recognize that no boy is worth forsaking a true friend. If you choose a romantic relationship over a friendship and the romantic relationship should come to an end, you'll find yourself wishing your friend was still around to support you.

2. A new friend is getting in the way. You may become upset if a friend of yours is spending less time with you after meeting someone else. Whether this "someone else" is a boyfriend or another girl, it's possible that you'll worry your friend prefers him or her to you. Jealousy can often lead to anger, so this type of situation has the potential to turn pretty nasty.

If you're ever faced with this type of problem, you must first remind yourself that no one can "steal" a friend. A friend is not something you own, like a cell phone or a piece of jewelry. A

SOME GREAT BOOKS FOR TEENS DEALING WITH FRIENDSHIP ISSUES

- *The Blue Girl*, by Charles de Lint
- *Breaking Point*, by Alex Finn
- *Dairy Queen*, by Catherine Gilbert Murdock
- *The Earth, My Butt, and Other Big Round Things*, by Carolyn Mackler
- *Speak*, by Laurie Halse Anderson
- *Stargirl*, by Jerry Spinelli

THE BLUE GIRL BY CHARLES DE LINT IS A NOVEL THAT FOLLOWS A CHARACTER, IMOGENE, AS SHE TRIES TO FIT IN AT A NEW HIGH SCHOOL.

friend is an independent human being who has the right to spend time with whoever she pleases. Also, just because a friend enjoys another person's company doesn't mean she cares less about you. No one can have too many friends. There's always room for everyone.

Of course, being a true friend does mean making sure you have enough time for everyone.

BECAUSE HARMING YOURSELF CAN'T POSSIBLY MAKE YOU HAPPY, GIVING IN TO PEER PRESSURE JUST DOESN'T MAKE SENSE. FEW THINGS ARE AS COOL AS A STRONG SENSE OF SELF-WORTH.

It's OK to hang out with different people every so often, but if you haven't seen a certain friend for quite some time, she may have a right to be upset with you. Make sure to give all your friends a piece of your time, and ask them to do the same for you.

3. Peer pressure takes over. Have you ever heard the phrase, "The more, the merrier"? This notion

can be what dictates peer pressure. People sometimes feel better about the bad things they're doing if other people are doing them, too. For example, a teenager who starts smoking cigarettes might feel guilty about her new habit. But if her friends start doing it with her, she'll at least feel she's not alone.

As a teenager, you're at an age when experimenting with harmful things like drinking and drugs is, unfortunately, commonplace. Some teens feel that by doing things they shouldn't, they are letting the world know they are their own bosses. At the same time, however, they're putting their grades, health, and friendships in jeopardy. So much for being good bosses to themselves!

If you find yourself being pressured by a friend, you may worry that if you don't do what she asks, you'll lose her companionship. What

ROMANCE FRIENDSHIP UNDERSTANDING COMMITMENT COMMUNICATION BOND FAMILY RELATIONSHIP

SOMETIMES, BEING A GOOD FRIEND MEANS LETTING THE OTHER PERSON KNOW THAT YOU'RE AFRAID SHE IS MAKING A BAD DECISION. JUST MAKE SURE TO BE SUPPORTIVE, NOT CONFRONTATIONAL.

you may not realize, however, is that a true friend would never ask you to do something to hurt yourself. Since holding on to a false friend is pointless, there's no reason for you to feel bad about saying no to peer pressure.

It could be that a friend of yours becomes the victim of peer pressure. If this should happen, try not to think of her as a bad person. Not everyone

is strong enough to avoid doing something unhealthy in an effort to fit in. However, this doesn't mean you should hold your tongue while your friend races down the wrong path. A good friend should want what's best for the other person, and in this case, what's best for your friend is that you let her know that she is making a big mistake.

ROMANCE FRIENDSHIP UNDERSTANDING COMMITMENT
COMMUNICATION
VING BOND FAMILY RELATIONSHIP

RESOLVING DISAGREEMENTS

Even if you keep the above advice in mind, you will never completely avoid having disagreements with your friends. Everyone has disagreements from time to time, no matter how good they are at handling relationships. If you and your friends do end up in an argument, there are some ways in which you can help put things to rest:

1. Force yourself to listen. No matter how wrong you think a friend may be, it's only fair to allow her to share her feelings. The only way you can expect her to listen to you is if you actively listen to her.

2. Change your shoes. In the previous chapter, you learned about how putting yourself in a family member's shoes can help end a disagreement. The same trick works with friends. If you look at a situation from a friend's point of view, you may be surprised to find she has a valid point. In addition, once she sees how willing you are to consider her side of things, she'll be compelled to do the same for you.

3. Keep it private. Asking mutual friends to take sides in an argument is equivalent to asking for trouble. Involving more people than necessary in a disagreement will only cause it to grow out of hand, and friends will rightfully see you as disloyal if you work to turn others against them.

Having a third party intervene in a dispute can be helpful, but only if that person is objective and experienced, like a school counselor.

Solving problems in a mature and healthy manner will help make your friendships stronger. Your friends will recognize that you care enough about them to do whatever it takes to keep your relationship positive. On the other hand, putting an end to toxic friendships, such as friendships in which the other person is pressuring you or showing you disrespect, will help you maintain your sanity. Not every friendship is meant to be, and if you have the strength to keep only those friends who are worth your time, you'll be much happier and healthier in the long run.

CHAPTER 4

BOY TALK

You and your peers are at a time when many of you may be embarking upon your first romantic relationships. These relationships are different from others in that they exist exclusively between two people. Usually, these two people possess a unique emotional connection and mutual desire for each other. Many teenage girls look forward to having a boyfriend so that they can take part in this special and thrilling experience. However, it's unnecessary to obsess over finding a significant other. Many young women who have been part of a couple will tell you that being single can be just as much fun. Being in a romantic relationship does have its advantages, but it also requires hard work and certain sacrifices.

Having a boyfriend means learning to understand the opposite sex. This task is never easy. Boys have a different way of looking at the world than girls do, so you can't always rely on them to relate to your point of view. Many of the problems that arise between couples have to do with the very different ways in which males and females communicate. For example, some girls worry that their boyfriends don't care about them because they rarely volunteer to share their feelings. What these girls forget is that, by nature, boys tend to be less emotionally expressive than girls. Therefore, when a boyfriend doesn't offer to tell you exactly how he's feeling, it doesn't necessarily mean he's heartless. Most likely, he's just being a guy.

Although it seems at times that males and females speak completely different languages, couples do need to make an effort to understand each other. Since you can't expect your boyfriend to react to things the same way you do, you'll have to learn to interpret his particular way of behaving in order to really know what's on his mind. A good boyfriend will do the same for you. He'll want to get to know you on such a level that he can tell how you're feeling just by looking at you. Achieving this kind of closeness takes time, but working toward it is a great exercise in building the strongest of relationships.

Even single girls can practice communicating with the opposite sex. Boyfriend or no boyfriend, you can always incorporate some boys into your circle of friends. The plus side to having boys as friends is that by becoming comfortable socializing with them in groups, you'll have an easier time spending time with them one-on-one.

When it comes to dating, boys are traditionally the ones who do the asking out. This doesn't mean, however, that you shouldn't ask a boy out yourself. In fact, doing so will only be beneficial to your dating record. Right away, the number of dates you go on will increase dramatically.

ROMANCE FRIENDSHIP UNDERSTANDING COMMITMENT COMMUNICATION WING BOND FAMILY RELATIONSHIP

MALES AND FEMALES HAVE VERY DIFFERENT WAYS OF COMMUNI-CATING. BUT HAVING A HEALTHY ROMANTIC RELATIONSHIP DOES NOT REQUIRE YOU TO SEE THINGS IN THE EXACT SAME WAY.

You may think that all the boys who are interested in you have already asked you out. This is never actually the case. Most boys are far too shy to approach you, and they will be relieved if you approach them instead. The only way to find out who these shy guys are is to ask boys out and see what they say.

You may be hesitant to address the opposite sex for fear of rejection. If so, you're not alone. Everyone—even

the most popular boy in school—agonizes over being rejected. Allowing this fear to cripple you, however, will do nothing to improve your love life. While you can expect to be met with rejection once in awhile, the only way to get someone to say yes to a date is to ask him in the first place.

It is important not to take rejection too personally. Teens don't always turn down dates just because they don't like the other person. Sometimes, they're simply too nervous to

Romantic relationships often have the potential to blossom into true love. However, even people in love must work hard to keep their relationship going strong.

DATING ROMANCE FRIENDSHIP UNDERSTANDING COMMUNICAT
GROWING BOND FAMILY RELATIONSHIP

give dating a shot. Other times, they may be dealing with a difficult breakup and aren't quite ready to date again just yet. If you get rejected, don't waste your time asking yourself why it happened. You'll probably never know the real reason. Instead, congratulate yourself on being brave enough to have taken a risk. If you are able to successfully face rejection, you won't be as afraid to ask for the things you want out of life and will consequently become more accomplished.

Once you do start dating, be careful not to let the intoxication of having a love life cloud your vision. Have you ever had a friend who found a boyfriend and then suddenly seemed to disappear? Some people become so wrapped up in having a significant other that they lose sight of everything else around them, including their friends. No matter how enamored you are with a guy, try not to become a "vanishing friend." Should your romantic relationship go sour, you'll want your friends by your side, and they'll be reluctant to support you if they feel you've been ignoring them.

Another thing you must keep an eye on while dating is your sense of self. Some young women make the mistake of allowing their romantic relationships to define them. They forget about their own interests and needs in order to concentrate completely on those of their significant other. Don't disrespect yourself by abandoning your individuality. You are a special person with her own hopes, dreams, and interests,

HAVING A BOYFRIEND CAN BE A VERY FULFILLING EXPERIENCE, BUT IT CAN ALSO BE CHALLENGING TO MAINTAIN A LIFE OUTSIDE OF YOUR RELATIONSHIP. BE SURE TO TAKE TIME FOR YOURSELF.

and these things must never be compromised in the name of a relationship.

It could be that at this time, you're just not interested in having a boyfriend. You either have too many other things on your plate, or you'd rather not have to deal with the drama that sometimes comes with having a significant other. Such an outlook is perfectly healthy. It's good to

have a positive attitude about being single. Not having a boyfriend gives you more time to focus on yourself and your needs. Unfortunately, many girls have the idea that life won't be complete until they have a boyfriend. This misconception not only brings down their self-esteem, it also prompts them to settle for less of a man than they deserve.

If you catch yourself pining for a boyfriend simply because you're lonely or depressed, stop it right there! A boyfriend is not a cure for either of these afflictions. In fact, the best way to have a happy and healthy romantic relationship is if you are first happy and healthy on your own first. Depending entirely upon a boyfriend for your sense of self-worth means that once you break up, your confidence level will at once be at a dangerous low.

When in a romantic relationship, it is vital that you take things slowly. Your romantic relationship will become much stronger if you take the time to really get to know the other person before doing things like kissing and having sex. Many teens move from one level of a romantic relationship to the next far too quickly. Girls sometimes worry that if they don't get physical with their boyfriends right away, they'll be dumped. They forget that being with someone who cares about them merely on a physical level isn't worth their time. A healthy romantic relationship should

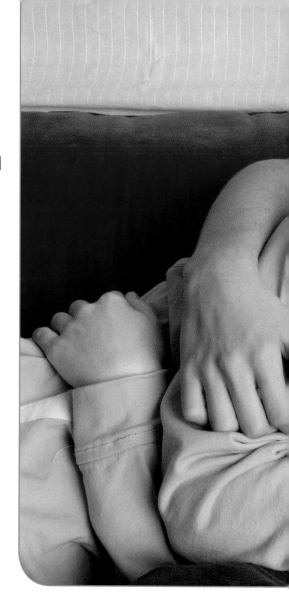

be more about caring and compassion than sexual activity. If a boyfriend is pressuring you to do things you aren't yet comfortable with, don't allow yourself to give in. A guy will be more likely to respect you if he sees that you value your body enough to move at your own pace. If he tells you differently, it's more than safe to assume that he isn't right for you.

TAKING A ROMANTIC RELATIONSHIP TO A PHYSICAL LEVEL SHOULD HAPPEN NATURALLY. IF ONE OF YOU FEELS UNCOMFORTABLE WITH THE WAY THINGS ARE PROGRESSING, THE RELATIONSHIP WILL LIKELY SUFFER.

Earlier, you read about the attributes that are necessary for the survival of any healthy relationship. One of these attributes was having a common goal. It's crucial to ask yourself from time to time whether you and your boyfriend seem to want the same thing out of your relationship. If you're ever not sure about the answer, the two of you may want to have a talk.

BREAKUPS

Unfortunately, many romantic relationships do come to an end. While you can never have too many friends, you can have only one boyfriend at a time, and you need to make sure you're with the one person who's best for you. No relationship is completely without problems, and it's normal for you and your boyfriend to have disagreements once in awhile. However, there are some very specific signs that point to a romantic relationship being ready to come to a close:

I. You want different things. Again, there's no point in prolonging a relationship in which there is no common goal. If one of you wants a long-term commitment and the other thinks you should consider your relationship no more than a summer fling, it's best to put an end to things on the spot. You may never see eye-to-eye on the matter, and sticking things out will only prolong an inevitable bad breakup.

BREAKUPS DON'T NEED TO BE NASTY. WHY MAKE A DIFFICULT SITUATION EVEN WORSE THAN IT ALREADY IS? IF YOU ARE FEELING TOO UPSET TO ENGAGE IN A MATURE DISCUSSION, WAIT TO FEEL BETTER BEFORE ACTUALLY BREAKING UP.

2. Your feelings have changed. It's common for a couple to lose the romantic feelings they once had for each other. People grow apart from their significant others, just as they grow apart from their friends. If you find yourself losing interest in your boyfriend, there's no need to feel guilty about it. Simply be honest about what you're feeling and bring up the possibility of the two of you parting ways. You may be tempted to stay in the relationship in an effort to see whether your romantic feelings come back to you, but it's unlikely that this will happen. Once you lose romantic interest in a person, it's almost impossible to naturally regain that interest. The best thing to do in this type of situation is to move on and not spend any additional time being a part of something that no longer excites you.

3. You're arguing constantly. No two people get along all the time, but if you and your boyfriend are fighting more than you are enjoying each other's company, something is amiss in your relationship. Constant quarreling doesn't mean that one of you is a negative person or that you should try harder to make things work. Usually, it just means that the two of you have grown apart and are therefore no longer able to relate to each other. It's best for this realization to lead to a breakup, as sticking with a relationship in which all you do is argue will only prolong the stress and hard feelings.

(continued)

♀ FORMER CELEBRITY COUPLES WHO HAD TO ENDURE BREAKUPS

No one is exempt from having his or her heart broken. Some of the most famous celebrities in the world have endured heartbreak. While breakups can be difficult initially, remember that you aren't alone in dealing with them. Celebrity couples who have had to endure public breakups include:

- Alexis Phifer and Kanye West
- Brad Pitt and Jennifer Aniston
- Guy Ritchie and Madonna
- Halle Berry and Eric Benet
- Joel Madden and Hillary Duff
- Miley Cyrus and Joe Jonas
- Nick Lachey and Jessica Simpson

BRAD PITT AND JENNIFER ANISTON WENT THROUGH A WIDELY PUBLICIZED DIVORCE IN 2005 AFTER FOUR YEARS OF MARRIAGE.

FRIENDSHIP UNDERSTANDING COMMITMENT
ROMANCE COMMUNICATION
LIVING BOND FAMILY RELATIONSHIP

4. Someone is behaving badly. Abuse and infidelity are never OK. If you are being abused or cheated on by a boyfriend, get out of the relationship before it destroys you. You absolutely deserve better, no matter what the circumstances.

Although breaking up is never easy, it's an unavoidable component to almost every romantic relationship. Fortunately, there are some steps you can take toward making sure your breakup is as painless as possible:

1. Do it in person. Because breaking up is so difficult to endure, some people prefer to do it over the phone or in an e-mail. However, initiating a breakup this way is considered cowardly and insensitive. Unless your soon-to-be-ex has hurt you in some way, it's important to show him that you still care for and respect him by breaking up in person. Only then will he be able to express his feelings to you and give you a proper good-bye.

2. Do it in private. Needless to say, breaking up when other people are around can be a humiliating experience. It is much more respectful to break up with someone in private.

3. Be honest. When breaking up with someone, you should never try to be hurtful. However, this doesn't mean you shouldn't be honest about why you want to end the relationship. The other person has the right to know why you feel the way you do. Some people try and lessen the

TEEN BOY AND GIRL RELATIONSHIPS: FACTS AND STATISTICS

- The rate of teen pregnancy has been slowly declining since the early 1990s.
- In 2001, a study showed that teen girls with abusive boyfriends were more likely to abuse drugs and alcohol and develop eating disorders.
- According to a 2008 survey, most teens reveal details about their romantic relationships to their friends but not their parents.
- In 2000, one in four teenage girls who had been in a romantic relationship reported having been pressured to engage in sexual intercourse.
- The number of teenage boys engaging in sexual intercourse has dropped significantly within the past fifteen years.

pain of a breakup by making empty promises, such as, "We can still be friends." Rarely do people ever mean such things, as being friends with an ex is almost as difficult as staying in a broken relationship. During a breakup, never make a promise you don't intend to keep. The other person will become angry once he finds out you were being untruthful.

4. Keep it short. Some couples turn a breakup conversation into a long-lasting debate. They rehash the relationship for days, weeks, or even months because they are too afraid to actually end it. With one party trying to

WHEN YOU FIRST BREAK UP WITH SOMEBODY, YOU MAY FEEL AS IF YOU'RE JUST TOO DEPRESSED TO BE AROUND OTHER PEOPLE. HOWEVER, HAVING FUN WITH FRIENDS IS A WELCOME DISTRACTION.

convince the other that they can still make things work, they break up and make up over and over, forcing themselves to endure a continuous cycle of pain.

When it comes to breaking up with someone, it's best to have it over and done with as soon as possible. When a relationship is no longer working, it's impossible to put it back together again for good.

DATING ROMANCE FRIENDSHIP UNDERSTANDING COMMUNICA GROWING BOND FAMILY RELATIONSHIP

Moving On

The actual breakup conversation is, unfortunately, only part of the breakup process. After breaking up with your boyfriend, you can expect to feel pretty miserable for awhile. However, you can also expect that things will get better. Although it may not seem like it at the time, it's possible to get over any breakup and be stronger for it in the end. In the meantime, here are some things you can do to lessen the pain:

1. Surround yourself with friends. Unless you've become a "vanishing friend," your friends will be around to support you through a breakup. The more you hang out with them, the more fun you will have, and the less your mind will wander back to your ex and "the way things were."

2. Don't overanalyze. It can be tempting for girls to replay a broken relationship over and over in

DATING AND RELIGIOUS BELIEFS

Most Western cultures are fairly lenient when it comes to teens spending time with the opposite sex. In mainly Muslim countries like Iran, this type of interaction is looked down upon, especially if a parent or guardian isn't present. Some Muslim teens living in Western countries have a hard time reconciling their religious backgrounds with their social lives. For example, if their friends are going to the movies or a party, they won't be able to go along if teens of the opposite sex will be present.

their heads in an effort to figure out exactly what went wrong. Doing this, however, is useless. The only thing you can know for certain after a breakup is that things just didn't work out. Don't torture yourself by trying to place blame. There are ups and downs in every relationship. When it ends, it's OK to let go without looking back.

3. Look on the bright side. There are positive aspects to any breakup, believe it or not. Once you're no longer part of a couple, you'll have more time for your friends. You'll also be able to reconnect with yourself and develop new hobbies and interests. And the best part is, once you're fully ready, you'll be free to meet a guy with whom you're more compatible.

Romantic relationships can be confusing at times, but they can also be extremely rewarding. Being a couple is an incredibly fulfilling experience, provided that both parties respect each other and want the same thing out of the relationship. It's a fact of life that love and pain sometimes go hand-in-hand, but if you have built strong, sturdy relationships with your friends and family, you will have plenty of people to help you through the hard times.

ROMANCE FRIENDSHIP UNDERSTANDING COMMITMENT COMMUNICATION
VING BOND FAMILY RELATIONSHIP

CHAPTER 5

YOUR OWN BEST FRIEND

Did you know you can actually have a relationship with yourself? It may sound strange, but of all the relationships you have, the one between you and yourself is the most important. You may be thinking, "But how can a relationship exist when there's just one person involved?" Well, the thing is, you can be two very different people at times.

Have you ever dressed a certain way just to fit in, or claimed to like a certain music group just because your friends were fans of theirs? If so, you know what it's like to not be true to yourself. In cases like these, it's as if there are two of you: the person you truly are, and the person you only appear to be.

Having a healthy relationship with yourself means being true to the person you really are. If you ignore this person, you will never be fully content. No matter how popular you become or what a loving boyfriend you have, a little voice inside of you will be asking, "Hey, what about me?"

FACTS ABOUT GIRLS AND SELF-ESTEEM

- Girls who are exposed to unrealistic images of women, such as airbrushed pictures of celebrities on magazine covers, are more dissatisfied with their bodies.
- Eating disorders, depression, and low self-esteem are the most common mental health problems in girls.
- Girls have a more difficult time dealing with stress than boys and are therefore twice as likely to be depressed by the age of fifteen.
- Studies show that today's teenage girls have less self-esteem than their parents had at their age.
- Diet and health have been cited as being the biggest concerns among teen girls, followed by sexual issues, skin problems, and drug and alcohol abuse.

Staying true to yourself while in high school can be tough. Often, the person you really are doesn't look or act like the people your peers look up to the most. You therefore push your true self to the back of your mind, making way for a new, more socially acceptable version of yourself. Making this move is almost never worth it. Experimenting with your personality is normal, but being someone you're not isn't.

Teens who aren't true to themselves almost always end up in trouble. In an effort to fit in, they submit to peer pressure and take on friends who don't really care about

IT'S FUN TO HAVE FRIENDS WITH WHOM YOU SHARE INTERESTS. BUT THAT DOESN'T MEAN YOU SHOULD WORK TO LIKE EXACTLY THE SAME MUSIC, MOVIES, AND BOOKS AS YOUR PEERS.

them. If they listened to their true selves more often, their futures would be much brighter. Your true self is smarter than you think. Most likely, she has better morals and aspirations than the other side of you—the person who just wants to be liked. By listening to her advice once in awhile, you could be doing yourself a big favor.

You may not realize it, but even the most popular, seemingly happy teens have issues with self-esteem. Being a teenager means undergoing a period of tremendous change. Changes are rapidly occurring to your body and mind, and you have new responsibilities. It's almost impossible to be comfortable and happy with yourself when you

ROMANCE FRIENDSHIP UNDERSTANDING COMMITMENT COMMUNICATION VING BOND FAMILY RELATIONSHIP

Believing in yourself provides you with the power to overcome many of life's obstacles. Therefore, working to build your self-esteem is an incredibly important task.

are constantly evolving. Feeling confused or upset about your identity doesn't mean you're inadequate or unworthy. It simply means you're a normal teenager facing normal teenage problems.

Some teens have a very difficult time dealing with their issues of self-esteem. They aren't sure how to develop confidence on their own, so they try and make themselves feel better by putting others down instead. This strategy never works. You may not know it to observe these people, but they usually feel pretty badly about the way they behave toward others. They therefore end up feeling even worse about themselves than they did before they started bullying.

Other teens try to boost their self-esteem by "fishing" for compliments. They say bad things about themselves in the presence of others, hoping these people will assure them they're wrong. This is another example of a useless technique for developing self-respect. No one likes to listen to someone whine and complain about themselves, so people who fish for compliments often don't accomplish more than persuading others to stay away from them.

BUILDING YOUR OWN SELF-ESTEEM

The only person who can effectively increase your self-esteem is you. Of course, when you're so used to putting yourself down, learning to build yourself back up again can require a concentrated effort. Here are some ways in which you can retrain yourself to think positively:

1. Pay yourself compliments. Admit it. You deserve a compliment once in awhile. Sadly, most teens spend so much time trying to convince themselves they're not good enough that they're soon unable to recognize their many positive qualities. Next time you start to insult yourself, try paying yourself a compliment instead. A teen who didn't get the role she wanted in the high school musical may try to convince herself she's untalented. What she should do, however, is compliment herself on being brave enough to try out in the first place. Not everyone has such courage. Another young woman may be upset over her low PSAT score. Her first instinct may be to tell herself she's unintelligent. However, she'd be better off if she patted herself on the back for being so passionate about her academics. Her deep desire to succeed will surely help her with her studies, resulting in a higher score the next time around.

2. Refocus on the positive. When you get home from school, instead of wincing over the bad things that happened to you that day, try making a list of the day's positive occurrences. You may be surprised to find that your time at school really wasn't as

CELEBRITIES AND THEIR MENTORS

- The forty-second president of the United States, Bill Clinton, was mentored by his high school band teacher, Virgil Spurlin.
- Media mogul Oprah Winfrey was mentored by her fourth grade teacher, Mrs. Duncan.
- Actor Leonardo DiCaprio looks to actor Robert De Niro as a mentor.
- R&B singer Usher's mentor was R&B legend James Brown.
- Actress Gwyneth Paltrow's mentor is pop super-star Madonna.

bad as you thought. Write down the negative notions as well. Take a look at this second list. Are the items included really worth agonizing over? If so, what can you do to improve your situation? It's no use being upset over something you're not planning on making better.

3. Have a plan. Certain things in life take work. No one becomes a stellar student, talented musician, or impressive athlete overnight. That said, if you're motivated enough, you can absolutely achieve greatness. Rather than just sitting around wishing you possessed a certain skill, create a concrete plan outlining the steps required for achieving it. At first, your plan may seem like a huge undertaking. It's possible that

you'll find it intimidating. However, once you get to work on it, before long, you'll be well on your way toward reaching your goal.

4. Survey your surroundings. Learn to be comfortable with taking an honest look at the people you surround yourself with. Are there friends or family members in your life who are constantly putting you down or not supporting your dreams? Your sense of self-worth may depend on your distancing yourself from such people. Remember, an uncaring relationship is never worth your time.

FINDING YOUR TRUE IDENTITY

Developing a positive relationship with your true self is all well and good, but what if you still aren't sure who that person is exactly? Again, it's normal for teenagers to not yet have a solid sense of self, so there's no reason to look down on yourself for feeling this way. In the meantime, here are some things you can do to get a better grasp on your true identity:

I. Spend quality time with yourself. Taking a look at your relationship with yourself probably isn't something you're used to doing. When you have so many other relationships to keep track of, it can be

WRITING IN A JOURNAL FORCES YOU TO CONCENTRATE AND THINK THINGS THROUGH. THE THOUGHTS YOU PUT DOWN ON PAPER ARE OFTEN MORE LOGICAL AND CONCRETE THAN THE THOUGHTS THAT RACE THROUGH YOUR HEAD.

FRIENDSHIP UNDERSTANDING COMMITMENT
ROMANCE COMMUNICATION
VING BOND FAMILY RELATIONSHIP

easy to forget about your own needs. Making other people happy is a noble goal, but if you don't take time for yourself, you won't have a good idea of who you really are and who you want to become.

Set aside some alone time each day and use it to further your quest of self-discovery. Listen to music, write in a journal, or simply close your eyes and relax. No matter what solitary activity you choose to engage in, if it's all for you, you'll be one step closer to becoming acquainted with yourself.

2. Find a mentor. A mentor is an older, more experienced person who can help you figure out your life's path. If you have a teacher, tutor, coach, or relative you look up to, ask her if she wouldn't mind talking to you about your future. Almost any adult would be honored to assist a younger person with her search for her true self and purpose. A mentor will share with you the lessons she's learned, mistakes she's made, and successes she's had in an effort to help you succeed. Working with a mentor will give you a better idea of what you want out of life and will consequently give you a better idea of who it is you want to be.

3. Conduct positive experiments. Experimenting with drugs and alcohol never yields positive results, but there are other perfectly healthy

If you truly want to connect with yourself, you'll need to set aside some time to be alone with your thoughts. Go for a walk, or sit in a place that makes you feel at peace.

FRIENDSHIP UNDERSTANDING COMMITMENT
ROMANCE COMMUNICATION
VING BOND FAMILY RELATIONSHIP

ways in which you can experiment with your image. For example, go ahead and try listening to a new type of music or dressing in a new sort of way, just to see how you like it. Neither of these activities are harmful to your health, after all. Just make sure, however, that you're experimenting for the sake of getting to know yourself, rather than trying to be like someone else.

4. Pay attention. On a daily basis, pay attention to how you react to things. What memories make you smile? Which conversations hold your interest? What are the subjects you catch yourself daydreaming about? Don't allow certain things to spark your interest, only to fade from your mind a moment later. Clues about your true identity pop up all the time in everyday life, so make sure to keep an eye out for them.

Getting to know yourself should be fun, not stressful, so don't feel pressured to figure out every detail of your being while in high school. Self-discovery is a lifelong process, especially since we undergo so many different changes as time goes on. There are certain aspects of yourself that are less likely to change, however, such as your values and morals. These aspects are especially worth paying attention to whenever you feel swayed by peer pressure.

Having a good relationship with yourself will actually improve your other relationships. When people see that you hold yourself in high regard, they'll be more likely to respect you. Being true to yourself will also make you a better communicator. If you know exactly what you want and how you feel, you'll have an easier time expressing yourself to others. Finally, if you love yourself the way you deserve to be loved, you'll be less likely to join up with those people who are unworthy of your time.

In the end, feeling good about yourself depends on you, and you alone. This is why it's a waste of energy to focus on getting others to accept you. You absolutely owe it to yourself to be your own best friend. If there's any one relationship that should always come out on top, it's your relationship with the wonderful person you are.

abuse An act of mental, physical, or emotional mistreatment.

ancestor A person from whom one is descended; a distant relative.

attribute A quality or characteristic.

berate To scold; rebuke.

common goal A shared objective between two parties.

communication The exchange of thoughts, opinions, and information.

compromise An agreement reached through an adjustment of conflicting ideas.

conundrum A perplexing problem.

crisis center A facility that provides intervention and other resources for those who are victims of a crisis.

empathy Identification with and understanding of another's situation, feelings, and motives.

exclusivity The agreement between a couple that they will only have a relationship with each other.

extramarital relationship A romantic relationship in which one of the parties is married to another person.

genealogy The study of family ancestries and histories.

identity The sense of self.

long-distance relationship A relationship between two parties who live a great distance from each other.

loyalty The state of being true to one's words, promises, vows, etc.

morals Motivation based on concepts of right and wrong.

peers People who are equal in age, rank, or class with another or others.

persona The role that one plays in public.

psychotherapist A trained professional who interacts with patients to initiate change in the patient's thoughts, feelings, and behavior through adaptation.

rehash To go back over; to discuss again.

relationship A connection between people.

resentment A lasting feeling of displeasure or ill will at someone or something.

self-esteem Your opinion of yourself, whether it be good or bad.

values Beliefs in which you have an emotional investment.

verbal abuse A type of abuse where the abuser uses words to cut down someone else.

American Counseling Association

5999 Stevenson Avenue

Alexandria, VA 22304

(800) 347-6647

Web site: http://www.counseling.org

This not-for-profit, professional, and educational organization is dedicated to the growth and enhancement of the counseling profession.

American School Counselor Association

1101 King Street, Suite 625

Alexandria, VA 22314

(800) 306-4722

Web site: http://www.schoolcounselor.org

The American School Counselor Association supports school counselors' efforts to help students' personal/social and career development.

Family Service Toronto

355 Church Street

Toronto, ON M5B 1Z8

Canada

(416) 595-9230

Web site: http://www.familyservicetoronto.org

This organization strengthens individuals, families, and communities through counseling and education.

National Domestic Violence Hotline

P.O. Box 161810

Austin, TX 78716
(800) 799-SAFE (7233)
Web site: http://www.ndvh.org
The National Domestic Violence Hotline provides domestic violence crisis intervention,
    safety planning, information, and referrals.

National Genealogical Society
3108 Columbia Pike, Suite 300
Arlington, VA 22204
(800) 473-0060
Web site: http://www.ngsgenealogy.org
This society promotes interest in the field of genealogy and family history.

RAINN: Rape, Abuse, and Incest National Network
2000 L Street NW
Washington, DC 20036
(202) 544-3064
Web site: http://www.rainn.org
RAINN is the world's largest anti—sexual assault organization.

Springtide Resources
215 Spadina Avenue, Suite 220
Toronto, Ontario M5T 2C7
Canada
(416) 968-3422
Web site: http://www.springtideresources.org

Springtide Resources promotes healthy and equal relationships, and works to prevent violence against women.

Stop Family Violence
311 West 57th Street, #518
New York, NY 10019
Web site: http://www.stopfamilyviolence.org
Stop Family Violence is an organization that is dedicated to empowering people to take action at the local, state, and national levels to ensure safety, justice, accountability, and healing for people whose lives are affected by violent relationships.

WEB SITES

Due to the changing nature of Internet links, Rosen Publishing has developed an online list of Web sites related to the subject of this book. This site is updated regularly. Please use this link to access the list:

http://www.rosenlinks.com/wom/rela

Anthony, Maggie, and Debra Beck. *My Feet Aren't Ugly!: A Girl's Guide to Loving Herself from the Inside Out.* New York, NY: Beaufort Books, 2007.

Burmingham, Sarah O'Leary. *How to Raise Your Parents: A Teen Girl's Survival Guide.* San Francisco, CA: Chronicle Books, 2008.

Canfield, Jack, and Mark Victor Hansen. *Chicken Soup for the Soul: Teens Talk About Family, Friends, and Love.* Cos Cob, CT: Chicken Soup for the Soul, 2008.

Dee, Catherine. *The Girl's Guide to Life: Take Charge of Your Personal Life, Your School Time, Your Social Scene, and Much More!* New York, NY: Little, Brown Young Readers, 2005.

Evans, Patricia. *Teen Torment: Overcoming Verbal Abuse at Home and at School.* Avon, MA: Adams Media Corporation, 2003.

Feuereisen, Patti. *Invisible Girls: The Truth About Sexual Abuse.* Berkeley, CA: Seal Press, 2005.

Harlan, Judith. *Girl Talk: Staying Strong, Feeling Good, Sticking Together.* New York, NY: Walker & Co., 2005.

Kirberger, Kimberly, and Colin Mortensen. *On Friendship: A Book for Teenagers.* Deer Beach, FL: HCI Teens, 2008.

Levy, Barrie. *In Love and in Danger: A Teen's Guide to Breaking Free of Abusive Relationships.* Berkeley, CA: Seal Press, 2006.

McCoy, Dorothy. *The Manipulative Man: Identify His Behavior, Counter the Abuse, Regain Control.* Cincinnati, OH: Adams Media, 2006.

McKay, Matthew, and Patrick Fanning. *Self-Esteem: A Proven Program of Cognitive Techniques for Assessing, Improving, and Maintaining Your Self-Esteem.* Oakland, CA: New Harbinger, 2000.

Shandler, Sara. *Ophelia Speaks: Adolescent Girls Write About Their Search for Self.* New York, NY: Harper, 1999.

Zimmerman Rutledge, Jill. *Dealing with the Stuff That Makes Life Tough: The 10 Things That Stress Teen Girls Out and How to Cope with Them.* New York, NY: McGraw-Hill, 2003.

Bliss, Beverly. "Step Families." *Parenthood in America*,
  1998. Retrieved February 4, 2009 (http://
  parenthood.library.wisc.edu/Bliss/Bliss.html).
Center for the Study of Long-Distance Relationships.
  "FAQs About Long-Distance Relationships." 2004.
  Retrieved February 4, 2009 (http://www.
  longdistancerelationships.net).
Discovery Health. "Teens and Self-Esteem." National
  Women's Health Resource Center. Retrieved
  February 5, 2009 (http://health.discovery.com/
  centers/teen/mentalhealth/esteem.html).
Family Guide. "Dating Violence Common Among Teens."
  Substance Abuse and Mental Health Services.
  Retrieved February 5, 2009 (http://www.family.
  samhsa.gov/teach/dating.aspx).
Family Guide. "Setting Rules for Teen Dating." Substance
  Abuse and Mental Health Services. Retrieved
  February 5, 2009 (http://www.family.samhsa.gov/
  set/dating.aspx).
Garofoli, Joe. "Teen Magazine Addresses Challenges of
  Being Muslim Girl in the United States." SFGate.com,
  June 18, 2007. Retrieved February 5, 2009 (http://
  www.sfgate.com/cgi-bin/article.cgi?f=/c/a/2007/
  06/18/MUSLIM.TMP).
Gurian, Anita. "How to Raise Girls with Healthy Self-
  Esteem." Education.com, NYU Child Study Center.

Retrieved February 4, 2009 (http://www.education.
com/reference/article/Ref_Mirror_Mirror_Wall).

Kuff, Nicolette. "New Survey Reveals Alarming Statistics
Related to Teen Relationships and Abuse." Blogger
News Network, 2008. Retrieved February 13, 2009
(http://www.bloggernews.net/116921).

Mahdi, Ali Akbar. "Fending for Themselves." *Iranian*,
2003. Retrieved February 5, 2009 (http://www.
iranian.com/AliAkbarMahdi/2003/August/Book).

New World Encyclopedia. "Extended Family." 2008.
Retrieved February 4, 2009 (http://www.
newworldencyclopedia.org/entry/Extended_family).

Passafuime, Rocco. "Leonardo DiCaprio." TheCinemaSource.
com. Retrieved February 13, 2009 (http://www.
thecinemasource.com/celebrity/interviews/
Leonardo-DiCaprio-This-Actor-s-Life-interview-374-0.html>).

Peterson, Karen. "Teenage Girls Setting Boundaries in
Relationships, Sex." *USA Today*, 2002. Retrieved
February 12, 2009 (http://www.usatoday.com/
news/health/child/2002-04-23-teen-sex.htm).

Sischy, Ingrid. "Matt and Ben—Interview with Matt
Damon and Ben Affleck, the Writers and Actors of
Goodwill Hunting." *Interview*, December 1997.
BNET.com. Retrieved February 13, 2009 (http://
findarticles.com/p/articles/mi_m1285/is_n12_v27/
ai_20078638/pg_7?tag=content;col1).

Study Guides and Strategies. "Active Listening." Retrieved
February 12, 2009 (http://www.studygs.net/
listening.htm).

TeenReads.com. "Ultimate Teen Reading List."
1997–2009. Retrieved February 4, 2009
(http://www.teenreads.com/features/ultimate-
reading-list.asp).

Who Mentored You? "Featured Celebrities." Retrieved
February 13, 2009 (http://www.hsph.harvard.edu/
chc/wmy2009/index.html).

About the Author

Bethany Bezdecheck is a writer for teens and a nonprofit professional living in the New York City area with her husband and dog. Her current passions include politics, bunny rabbits, independent films, artisan cheeses, jewelry-making, and learning to speak Romanian.

Photo Credits

Cover © www.istockphoto.com/iofoto; pp. 6–7 © Reuters/Corbis; pp. 12–13, 42–43, 52–53 Shutterstock.com; pp. 14–15 © J. Birdsall Social Images/Custom Medical Stock Photo; pp. 16–17 © www.istockphoto.com/Miodrag Gajic; pp. 18–19 © David Bacon/The Image Works; pp. 20–21 © www.istockphoto.com/Jeanell Norvell; pp. 24–25 © Solus-Veer/Corbis; p. 29 Yellow Dog Productions/Taxi/Getty Images; pp. 30–31 © www.istockphoto.com/RonTech2000; pp. 34–35 © Robert Llewellyn/Corbis; pp. 36–37 © John Henley/Corbis; p. 39 Steve Mason/Photodisc/Getty Images; p. 47 © www.istockphoto.com/Willie B. Thomas; pp. 50–51 © www.istockphoto.com/Alberto Pomares; pp. 54–55 © www.istockphoto.com/Igor Balasanov; pp. 58–59 © T. Bannor/Custom Medical Stock Photo; pp. 60–61 © www.istockphoto.com/Galina Barskaya; pp. 66–67 © www.istockphoto.com/Steve Pepple; pp. 68–69 © www.istockphoto.com/Chris Schmidt; pp. 70–71 © www.istockphoto.com/Kevin Russ; pp. 72–73 © Estelle Klawitter/zefa/Corbis; pp. 74–75 © www.istockphoto.com/ericsphotography; p. 77 Kevin Winter/Getty Images; pp. 80–81 © www.istockphoto.com/Aldo Murillo; pp. 86–87 Ron Levine/Taxi/Getty Images; pp. 88–89 © www.istockphoto.com/Michael Krinke; pp. 92–93 © www.istockphoto.com/Christine Glade; pp. 94–95 © www.istockphoto.com/VMJones.

Designer: Nicole Russo; Editor: Bethany Bryan; Photo Researcher: Amy Feinberg